I0845710

Julio M. Shiling

Latin America Under Socialist Siege

BY THE SAME AUTHOR

Dictatorships and Their Paradigms: Why Do Some Dictatorships Fall While Others Do Not?

Democratization in Cuba: A Concise Manual

11J, Exoduses, Embargo, and Martí in Cuba

Espionage, Accomplices, and Other Instruments of Castroism

China: The Monster Made in the West

Things to Know About Politics

American Exceptionalism: Creed, Culture, and Politics

Latin America Under Socialist Siege

Trump: Candidacy, Presidency, and Persecution

The Marxist Insurrection in America

The Tampered 2020 Election: Unfair and Spurious

The Biden-Obama Regime: A Fabian Path to Socialism

Ukraine: A Fight for Freedom and Sovereignty

Islamism: Enemy of Liberty

DEDICATION

For Marina, sharing the dream and hope that the Americas,

from one end to the other, will be free and democratic

ACKNOWLEDGMENT

Gratitude in the biggest proportions goes to Jose Tarano for the painstakingly effort to make this project possible.

CONTENTS

PREFACE

LATIN AMERICA UNDER SOCIALIST SIEGE

Latin America has been besieged by communism since the Bolsheviks came to power. The Communist International (Comintern), created in 1919, officially launched Marxism-Leninism's global war for power. When Castro-Communism established the Soviet beachhead in the Western Hemisphere, not a single Latin American country was spared from the Marxist attempt to seize political control. The fall of the USSR did not change that offensive. It only changed the imperial leadership of the Soviet Union to Cuba and the methodology for subverting the established order. The financing of this new phase of the socialist war has been done with Venezuelan oil, drug, and information trafficking and the leasing of a neo-slavery force, particularly the medical service brigades.

This work explores this development through a collection of writings. Specific country cases are examined. The Sao Paulo Forum, heir to the Comintern, initiated in 1990 a new way of undermining republican institutions in order, once in power, to proceed with their systemic dismantling. Typically, the cases that succeeded in repelling this new

Marxist strategy never eliminated the danger, as recent cases in Brazil, Argentina, Chile, Bolivia, and Colombia remind us. The war to make the Americas communist continues. The democratic nations of the region, especially the United States, must take a more proactive approach if freedom is to have a home in the Americas.

CHAPTER 1 ARGENTINA

Argentina: A Nation Under Siege (1955-2006)

When Ana María González visited her friend María Graciela Cardozo's house to place the bomb on her schoolmate's father's bed that hours later would blow the brains out of the Buenos Aires police chief, did she imagine that she would still have 27 more years to go before achieving power? The horrible murder committed by the Montonero teenager on June 16, 1976, typified the indiscriminate violence unleashed to promote the Marxist premise of the class struggle that, formally, had begun at that moment.

Today, 3 years after the 2003 elections and 48 years since John William Cooke, an activist of hybrid nationalist-Marxist-Leninist ideas, began in September 1955 the "Peronist Resistance," the war to implant communism in the homeland of San Martín, we see the Argentine Republic increasingly heading towards its sterilization as a free society. Before entering into the examination of the past and the presidency of Néstor Kirchner in Argentina, a review of the facts is mandatory to see how they occurred and the ideas that sustain that trajectory that today enjoys the officialist apogee.

Discussing the merits of Marxism as an abstract concept is not the purpose of this article, however, a basic understanding of it is fundamental to understand the process that Argentina (and other places) has lived and is living. Marxism, like National Socialism (Nazism), are deterministic ideologies. They see the development of the world as following "laws" that manifest themselves through "struggles." Nazism interprets supposed "laws of nature" as materializing in a "struggle of races." For Marxism, everything follows the "laws of history" which unfold in a "class struggle."

The adherents of these doctrines consider themselves as agents in charge of assisting these "processes," translated by them as immutable. Hence, the Nazis used the practice of eliminating the non-Aryan as a meritorious collaboration with nature. Communists also embrace the practice of extermination, in this case of classes (social, political, religious, cultural or ideological), as a prerequisite for, together with the alteration in the relations of production, reaching the end of "alienation," the utopian port of the Marxist boat and building the "new man."

Marx virulently expressed the need to merge violence with all revolutionary action. His contempt for pacifism is notorious. Revolutionary armed struggle, intending to violently overthrow capitalist systems, was not only consistent with Marx's ideas, but necessary. And the Argentines, who believed and fought to implement the communist paradigm, did not commit heresy with that pseudo-religion that is Marxism. They were faithful to the methodology prescribed by its founder.

The struggle to turn Argentina into a socialist republic (not to be confused with Social Democracy) has had six periods. The actors were an amalgam of Marxist-Leninist movements which, although sometimes evidencing antagonisms between their fractions, all conspired in favor of the conversion of Argentina into a communist state. In the end, they ended up reconstituting or merging into two: the People's Revolutionary Army (ERP) and the Montoneros. The first stage (1955-1968) consisted mainly of rural guerrilla groups in notorious areas of the country such as the provinces of Tucumán, Salto, and other mountainous areas. The armed subversive action was unsuccessful in its attempt to achieve a convincing victory.

The second stage, from 1969 to 1972, marked an intensification of the Marxist war by incorporating urban guerrillas into the insurgency. This massive inclusion of the cities raised the level of the belligerent contest. The kidnapping, torture, and assassination in May 1970 of former president Pedro Aramburu by the Montoneros warned of a bloody decade ahead for Argentina. The remarkable efforts of the security forces to stop the subversive offensive led to the establishment of a legal framework to combat the communists, such as the Federal Criminal Chamber. This legal instrument served to prosecute and convict more than 2,000 terrorists.

The return of democracy in May 1973 marked the beginning of the third period (1973-1976) of the communist war for Argentine state power. Theoretically, democracy, as a political system, is a staunch enemy of doctrinal schemes such as Marxism-Leninism, which employs totalitarianism as its mode of operation. However, the will to destroy the communist onslaught for the new president, Héctor Cámpora, seems not to have been present. The first official act of the newly inaugurated president was to repeal the Federal Criminal Chamber. This frontal attack on the legal mechanism to confront terrorism and the subsequent amnesty for all the terrorists who had been convicted vitalized the antisystem movements. Cámpora also dismantled the Supreme Court and handed over the University of Buenos Aires, in the capacity of virtual interventionist, to the notorious communist Rodolfo Puiggros (later to become a Montonero leader). Subversion was galvanized.

Assassinations, kidnappings, bombings, attacks on garrisons, banks, etc., reached unprecedented levels. On July 13, Cámpora resigned. This was something that many expected and considered his presidential feat as a premeditated prelude to the return of Juan Domingo Perón to power. New elections were called for September, which Perón won with 61% of the vote. Considering the Peronist roots of the Montonero movement, Perón (and many of those who voted for him) thought that the subversive movement would find, in the mentor, a balm for appeasement. Perón, like Cámpora before him, underestimated the appetite of those committed to establishing nothing less than a Marxist order in Argentina. All efforts to co-opt subversion (and there were many) proved fruitless. The grand marshal of Argentine statism, Juan Domingo Perón, was abandoned by those who, emerging from his fascist-socialist ranks, found in communism, a more palatable variant of socialism. The caudillo did not silence their anger.

Perón's answer to the Marxist subversive war was the Triple A. This organization, operating illegally and clandestinely, began a furtive campaign to penetrate Marxist subversive cells and neutralize their members. With only nine months in power, Perón passed away, far from having lessened or, much less, annihilated his new enemies, former disciples. His wife, Isabel Martínez de Perón, remained as president.

Isabel Perón's presidency began with great aggressiveness in the fight against the revolutionary war that she maintained in this third period, which culminated in 1976 with a military coup. At the beginning of 1975, Operation Independence was authorized (secret decree No. 261), a campaign granting broad powers to the Argentine army to combat the communist guerrillas in Tucumán, a province heavily beaten by the ERP and threatened with becoming a "liberated zone."

The merciless cruelty exercised by the Marxists in the war was typified by the discovery, in 1975, of the body of Lieutenant Colonel Larrabure, kidnapped for more than a year, confined to a pit called "people's prisons," dug under a Larrabure house. He had lost forty kilos during his captivity and his corpse showed a rectangular contusion in the shape of a hammer, in the neck he had a strangulation groove by backward twisting and, in the genital organs, inflammatory congestion, like that caused by electric shocks. The terror and national indignation before the red barbarism reached unbridled proportions.

Despite the efforts of Isabel Perón's government to curb the subversive advance, in addition to Operation Independence and decree No. 2772 of October 1975, giving greater powers to the armed forces to deal with the insurgency, the chaos did not seem to weaken. The fact is that the Argentine authorities, after Cámpora's decree repealing the Federal Criminal Chamber and the amnesty law pardoning more than 2,000 terrorists, never regained the ground by winning over the communist warriors. It is no coincidence that more than 52% of the terrorist acts and 70% of the assassinations were carried out during democratic periods, between 1973 and 1976.

The fourth period (1976-1979) of the war follows the military coup of March 1976. It was called a "military coup" because of the ascendancy to the executive of the

Argentine state of the military junta headed by Jorge Videla, Massera, et al. and the non-democratic way it was achieved. But in reality, it was, rather, a civil-military coup, since there was popular demand for the intervening praetorian action, and it had the broad backing of most of the multi-party legislative and judicial branches of the Argentine nation. Civil society, overwhelmingly, reinforced morally and with generous enthusiasm, the military action. This included leftist personalities such as Jacobo Timmermann, Ernesto Sábato, etc., with the latter paying impressive praise to the "liberator" Videla. Had free elections been held at that time in the face of the existing crisis, with great probability, he would have obtained perhaps the most decisive majority in the history of Argentine elections.

The mission of the 1976 military junta was to neutralize the Marxist offensive, its terrorist actions, and to put an end to the project of establishing a communist republic in South America. Their concern was not to win popularity contests, and that was undoubtedly a major strategic mistake. The challenge they faced was enormous. At the time, the Marxist fighters represented the largest insurrectionary force in the Western Hemisphere. Their unconventional way of waging guerrilla warfare, rural and urban, made the task of fighting them difficult. Despite the ferocity and power of the ERP, the Montoneros, the Castro-Communist tyranny, international communism, the radical left and their respective sympathizers, the Argentine security forces won, in three years, the war and reestablished order.

The Marxist-Leninist struggle for power, with its use of armed terror, took place between 1955 and 1979. It's cost to Argentine society was enormous. This atrocious war to impose a system on the majority, by an elitist and fanatical minority, which obeyed a radical, atheistic, and intolerant ideology, collectivized mourning and chaos. Between 1969 and 1979 alone, there were 21,642 terrorist acts executed by the communists! The crushing military defeat suffered by the Marxist fighters led the subversive leadership to change the battlefield. The military regime's disregard for the claim of images and perceptions proved, in the end, to be a colossal mistake that the enemy capitalized on.

The fifth stage (1980-2003) covers the final part of the military mandate. After winning the war in 1979, it goes through the return to democracy with the presidencies of Raúl Alfonsín, Carlos Menem and concludes with the rise to power of the current president. The Argentine Marxist leadership and its internationalist revolutionary accomplices did not cease in their conspiratorial efforts to establish a socialist dictatorship in the land where Sarmiento was born. The methodology to conquer power, with the doors of the armed road closed, turned out to be the terrain of public opinion in the capitals of the capitalist western world.

The red war publicity embraced the dissemination premise of Hermann Goebbells, Hitler's Minister of Propaganda, that repeating a lie enough times and converting it into public opinion, makes it a "truth." The project was to turn the victimizers into victims. The victimization, it was hoped, would generate a worldwide reaction that would put pressure on the victors of the armed war to relinquish power. And the space established, the usurper task would give, in national territory, a new impetus.

The issue of the "disappeared" turned out to be an ingenious scheme, within a very well elaborated instrumentation, to facilitate the road to power. In political lexicon, the act of "disappearing" someone consists of the detention and execution, without trial and unofficially, of a real or imaginary opponent. Yes, unfortunately and without a doubt, there were disappearances in Argentina. Of course, they were not the bombastic and hyperinflated numbers offered by the defenders of Marxist subversion. Serious figures vary between 4,000 and 7,706. A task complicated by the constant reappearance of people considered "disappeared" who, however, were living and active in Europe, Latin America, and the former socialist countries. Subsequent compensations to relatives ensure that the numbers will never amount to real proportions.

The systematic practice of arresting and executing combatants without legal review was carried out by Argentine governments, both democratic and non-democratic, during the 1970s. This activity intensified with the military intervention of 1976 and lasted until 1979. However, the pre-military coup disappearances do not seem to have concerned them much. This has been a strategic omission.

The Argentine public authorities, using the mechanization of unofficially apprehending and killing captured subversive forces, put an end to the war. The counter-offensive launched by the government, and the military regime in particular, neutralized the armed pursuit of power by the Marxists. Its members and sympathizers abandoned the armed route and opted for mechanisms operating in open societies (the same ones they would annihilate if they had come to power).

The new battlefield was international public opinion. Nothing could be easier than to victimize those who lost the war. It does not matter if they were the ones who started it. The intense victimization campaign needed "victims" and "villains." Those who escaped abroad with international communism and their accomplices on the left, spectacularly choreographed the psychological onslaught.

As a methodology, it would be obligatory to decontextualize history. The practice of decontextualizing is a cunning lie. That way, there would be a clear "villain." They removed, from the long process of anti-subversive struggle, the period after the military coup of 1976, ignoring 21 previous years of constant military confrontation with the antisystem forces. This is how the theme of the "disappeared" was developed. The shameless art of decontextualizing, of making a parenthesis of only a stretch of history and pretending that it has no organic links, of making believe that all the violence arose from the military coup and that they (the insurgents) "responded" to that act, was only possible due to disinformation, ineptitude, ignorance, and ideological conditioning.

By artificially maneuvering through legal channels and legitimate institutions, they managed to dodge attention from their criminal past. Serious organizations, particularly human rights organizations, were cajoled into canonizing groups that until previous days had committed acts of the same magnitude as the one they were now pointing out. The Falklands fiasco returned Argentina to democracy. At that moment, the mutilation of the legality of accommodation to satisfy their ideological agenda began.

The electoral victory of Raúl Alfonsín, politician of the Radical Civic Union (UCR) and former lawyer of Mario Santucho, notorious terrorist leader of the ERP, extended the advertising contest to Argentine territory. The aim of socializing Argentina found a very comfortable environment facilitated by the Alfonsín administration. The way of a biased and ideologically directed legality was immediately put into practice. Decree No. 158/83 institutionalized the historical and legal decontextualization. This executive order criminalized what was committed during the war, mostly only by one side (the public forces) and for a specific period (during the military regime). The 359 disappeared of 1975, the 549 of the first semester of 1976 and all those committed by the Triple A, Perón's (Juan D.) paramilitary gang, did not interest the partisan inquisitors. It was obvious that the officialist magnifying glass would not be remotely interested in investigating the atrocities committed by the revolutionary ex-combatants.

The strategy of selective disappearances received domestic officialdom with Decree No. 187/83, which established the CONADEP, a commission heavily committed to the purposes of the ex-insurgents. This instrument full of errors, omissions and falsehoods served as the basis for Alfonsinist "justice." Soon after, the trials of the military officers who stopped the armed Marxist war began.

The Alfonsín government obtained, for the Argentine Marxist terrorists, their supporters and the radical left, impressive achievements. Offering the podium of a democratic regime, it legitimized before the public opinion, the complaints of the defeated subversives and covered up their barbaric crimes. For most Argentines, impoverishment under his rule was not only moral and cultural.

In his eagerness to socialize the country, Alfonsín almost destroyed Argentina by nationalizing, by 1985, half of the national means of production, collapsing economic growth, productivity, purchasing power and real wages. What was on the rise were prices, crime, real unemployment, and inflation. The latter at carnivalesque low levels, which punished the neediest most severely. Despite the generous concessions granted by Alfonsín to the Marxists and the socializing immersion of his gesture, the conspirators seem not to have been satisfied.

Faithful to their doctrinal preaching, the communists resumed the war offensive by attacking, in 1989, the military regiment in La Tablada. As a military campaign, it was disastrous for the communists. The public forces immediately managed to crush the attack. Defending the nation and repelling the cowardly assault, more than 10 Argentines died, including Major Fernandez Cutiellos, killed with a bullet to the face after having his tongue and testicles cut off. Sadly, before the end of the next decade, communist murderers would be walking the streets free.

The rise of Carlos Saul Menem marked an obstacle to the aims of achieving a socialist and Montonero Argentina. However, undeniable corruption (Argentina's non-partisan problem), selective business concessions, excessive public spending and cloudy political agreements, the socialist advances in the political, cultural, and legal spheres achieved, courtesy of the previous administration, were a step backwards. The quasi-liberal scheme, the rapprochement with the U.S., the condemnation of Castro-Communism in public forums and the pardoning of war participants on both sides, searching for national reconciliation, momentarily derailed the Marxist momentum in Argentina.

Unfortunately, Menem's links with Peronism and its socio-political machinery, the structural reversions to antisystem programming's remained incomplete and mediatized. This atrophied the potential Argentine take-off, and much remained in the swamps of the socialist counterculture. Those who came after, not only continued the misreading and misapplication of the liberal creed but offered the conspiratorial forces the greatest opportunity in a decade to achieve power.

The political lexicon degraded to shameful levels, blaming foreign powers, their institutions and economic model, instead of assuming the ineptitude of Creole politicians who did not know how to manage the impressive wealth acquired or control public waste, resurfacing the premise of inviting the state to expand its power, slanderously blaming a theoretical paradigm that was never practiced.

Antisystem movements quickly mobilized to break the democratic order and undermine political harmony. The expression of social discontent was hijacked by extremists who decided to redefine "democracy." Fernando De La Rúa, with his resignation, gave the mobs and their henchmen a new format to attain power. Even the act of commuting the sentence of the La Tablada attackers did little to pardon him for the unforgivable event for the radical left of condemning the Castro regime in the UN Human Rights proceedings, despite Cuba having the infamous "distinction" of being the country with the highest number of political prisoners per capita in the world and being a faithful and consistent practitioner of systematic torture.

Politicians such as Eduardo Duhalde, one of the interim presidents, returned to the unscrupulous routine of refusing to cast the Argentine vote in the dignified column of nations that condemned communist Cuba at the UN. Undoubtedly, gestures like that, the release from prison of notorious terrorists, such as Gorriarán Merlo (the closing act of the Duhaldist mandate) and the extension of ideological clientelism, pointed out that the Marxist locomotive was back on track. Thus ended the fifth period of the revolutionary struggle for Argentine power.

The new methodology of victimizing the aggressors by distorting history to institutionalize the counterculture (Marxist premise), protected by a partisan legality (a tactic of struggle exercised by the Argentine Marxists after their defeat in the war field) found, in the rise of Néstor Kirchner, its raison d'être and marked the sixth and current period of the communist siege (2003 – present).

With 22% of the popular vote (the lowest in Argentina), Kirchner came to power. In a "Trojan horse" that entered through the door of a weakened democracy and inserted Montonerism in the Argentinean state leadership. What the bombs, assassinations, kidnappings, tortures, and terror in general did not achieve, was made possible by the Machiavellian strategy adopted at the end of the armed conflict.

Two phenomena of modernity have made it easy for radical elements to acquire power. The first, the inclusion of private property, intimidated and co-opted, into socialist praxis. The second, the use of democracy itself, as a system for attaining power. Communism is an end, not a means. To achieve this utopia, the operative mode is to implant authoritarianism and then, depending on the extremity of the purposes, if necessary, to exercise totalitarianism. The metamorphosis that Marxism has undergone by incorporating variants of capitalism, i.e., concessionary capitalism, mercantilism, etc., tolerating private property schemes to enlist it in concept and practice, in its notions of production relations (as explained by Deng Xiao Peng in 1978 and practiced by Lenin in 1921), paved the doctrinal way for socialists like Kirchner. By establishing gray areas, the veracity of intentions has been easier to conceal. Additionally, the inability of socialism to solve the needs of its inhabitants has engendered a relationship of irremediable dependence on capitalism. It is this condition of inveterate parasitism that forces the tolerance of private property, even when, dogmatically, it despises it.

The use of the democratic forum to reach the ruling elite is the second factor. Typically, facing difficulty in taking possession of the government by force of arms, the democratic path is another method of taking over the state. So did Hitler and National Socialism. Monopolizing power is the goal. The obstacles are civil society and the opposition. Undoubtedly, this process of consolidation of power, when the dictatorship in formation is part of democracy, becomes more difficult. Unfortunately, this phenomenon is repeating itself all too often. The Marxists in Argentina, since May 25, 2003, with an ex-Montonero president ruling from the Casa Rosada, have been doing so.

Kirchner's inauguration was attended by the most favored figures of the radical left. There was the tyrant-in-chief Fidel Castro, receiving the distinction of having the longest meeting with the new president. His disciple Hugo Chávez also rubbed elbows with the honoree. This quasi-summit of terrorists, dictators, their apologists, and parrots was not a mere publicity "show," as some deluded people suggested. Kirchner quickly demonstrated the seriousness of his convictions.

Former Montoneros overflowed Kirchner's cabinet. Rafael Bielsa was given the Ministry of Foreign Affairs; Carlos Kunkel was assigned the Undersecretary of the Presidency; Enrique Albistur was entrusted with the Secretariat of Communication; Eduardo Sigal was made Undersecretary of American Integration; Eduardo L. Duhalde was appointed Secretary of Human Rights. Duhalde was appointed Secretary of Human Rights; Juan Carlos Dante Gullo, Presidential Advisor; Jorge Taiana was appointed Secretary of Foreign Affairs; Patricia Vaca Narvaja was appointed Secretary of Consumer Defense; Juan González Gaviola was assigned to be interventionist of PAMI; Carlos

Bettini, Ambassador to Spain and, more recently, Minister of Defense Garré. All of them ex-Montoneros. With this structural composition it was clear that in this regime the hegemony would be Montonero.

The mechanisms with the capacity to stop or destroy the projects of the new administration of ex-subversives were quickly confronted. The Armed Forces immediately saw the removal of 52 high-ranking officers from their command. New officers with ideological affinities or opportunistic weaknesses were put in place. The intelligence services, necessary to defend a modern nation, were fatally weakened. Opponents, for Marxists, are not only the real ones, but also the imaginary and potential ones. A slanderous smear campaign (greater than those of the past) was set up. A series of legalities, traps, and reinterpretations were dispatched to supplement the planning measures.

Decrees with established precedents, such as Due Obedience and Punto Final, designed to heal the wounds of a difficult war, were reversed. The intent was clear, in addition to the vindictive spirit, Kirchner strengthened the purpose of domesticating the institution with the greatest possibility of blocking the march to despotism. The intention is softening enough for the uniformed to respond, not to the Homeland, but to the Party.

Propagandistically, the counterculture that Montonerismo fought to institutionalize requires the alienation of the Armed Forces. The hidden premise of repealing the prohibition to extradite Argentine officers to third countries, obeys the clear objective of intimidating the military forces by enlisting, through international complicity, Marxist judges willing to prosecute foreigners, having in their backyard, paradoxically, terrorists like Santiago Carrillo to imprison. The Spanish communist (Carrillo) ordered the massacre of more than 5,000 people in less than three months, during the Spanish Civil War. This psychological dismemberment is intended to instill terror within the military.

The monopolization of power requires intolerance not only of opponents, but also of dissidents. The Argentine state, being the largest single employer, the task of punishing, threatening or rewarding plays perfectly into Kirchner's dictatorial pretensions. An example was the mass dismissal of Daniel Scioli's allies when the vice president questioned the "seriousness" of the new regime. The expulsion of Dr. Sanchez Herrera, Treasury Attorney, for having legally represented General Juan Bautista Sasiain, is another example (the former lost his father and the latter, his sister, in terrorist acts). This is gross brazenness, when its minister, no less than the Secretary of Human Rights, is not only an ex-terrorist, but was the legal representative of Mario Santucho, founding assassin (mentioned above) of the ERP, indicted for the kidnapping, torture and murder of Sallustro, manager of Fiat.

The judicial branch is today a mere ornament that the Montonero regime uses to seal its internal deliberations, masking its almost complete power. The Tocquevillian notion of "separation of powers" is, in today's Argentina, a mirage. Judges fulfilling their functions, but who have not coincided with the socialist administration, particularly in the Supreme Court, through intimidation or direct threat, have resigned, been fired, or co-opted. In their place, new judges, adept at Montonero fundamentalism, have been placed, ready to dispense "revolutionary justice." This very dangerous development facilitates the absolutist solidification of the Kirchnerist regime, as it can define and prescribe what is "legal" and "constitutional."

With the subordination of the judicial branch, the practice of censorship has risen to alarming proportions. Legal terminology such as "coup preaching," "apology of crime" and "protection of the constitutional order" have been incorporated into the legal codes of today's Argentina. None of them, if there were a truly competent judicial system, would survive in a genuine democracy.

With the sterilization of the Armed Forces and the Courts achieved, the task of disintegrating civil society was simplified. Having the ability to "legalize" and reinforce the ostracism it promotes and the inability to reverse the unconstitutionality of such action, elementary freedoms have been disappearing. The effect is that of a velvet censorship. The population en masse, broken by intimidation, desists from effective and frontal confrontations against the Kirchnerist regime. Front organizations, set up to give the image of "popular support" and serve as shock forces to counteract social discontent, are the ideological patrols of the Montoneros. The piqueteros, radical movements and co-opted unions are some of the structures that serve as a false image for the outside world while acting as pressure agents inside the country.

Information media, integrally committed to the socialist officialdom, deal with the dejection of the Church and any other non-third world denomination. Propagandists linked to the Kirchnerist government unload their lead incessantly to propagate the discrediting of institutions that embrace the belief in God. They use all the weight of the servile press, seeking to culturally root atheism. They censor, ridicule, isolate and intimidate to impose a social price on Argentine society for believing in and worshiping the Supreme Being. The fundamentalist atheism that conditions communism, prescribes, without equivocation, such proposition. The pseudo-religion that is Marxism makes irreconcilable its coexistence with a vibrant Church that refuses to be an accomplice. Verbitsky, the Argentine Goebbells, and so many others at the service of the Montonero regime, know this very well. That is why, so ruthlessly, they fight it.

The explosive enlargement of the public sector, which has taken place in the last three years, is part of the scheme designed to automate civil society. The nationalization of Argentina is, in its maximum expression, the arrival at the nirvana of collectivism. More power to the state comes at the expense of the individual. The concentration of the economy in public hands does not translate into enrichment of the "people." That lie has been cynically sold to them. The "people" do not become owners of anything, they remain marginalized from decisions and are clearly at the mercy of what is in the storehouse of ideas inside the heads of those who control power.

A democracy, to be genuine, requires pluralism. Decentralization of political and economic power are firm barriers to prevent despotism. The sovereignty of a society resides, not with those who govern, but with the governed. That is why, with frantic impetus, this administration seeks the regulatory grandiloquence granted by a predatory state to, in this way, concretize its hegemony over the detail in the life of each Argentinean. A wonderfully perverse and prerequisite mechanism to implement the goal for which they have been fighting since 1955: a socialist Argentina.

At present, the public institutions most capable of preventing the penetration of communism, such as the Armed Forces and the Supreme Court, are defenestrated. The political opposition remains disorganized. On the civilian side, the Church is besieged by the official counterculture and, with very noble exceptions, seems to prefer to wait for the development of events. The private sector, the engine truly capable of producing wealth, is increasingly regulated and frightened. The only sign of liberalization is the unpunished license given to criminals, many of whom are on the state payroll.

Does this government have the legitimacy to do what they are doing? That in its first election it won with 22% of the vote and 39.5% in the second leaves doubts if the concept of the majority vote is to be believed. The hired mobs are the face that Montonerismo presents in the face of this unknown. They want to make believe that mob rule and "democracy" are synonyms.

Is all lost? No. It is up to Argentines to break the silence and not play along with this dictatorship under construction. The Kirchnerian dynasty is already maneuvering. Clientelism, through decriminalization and criminal tolerance, promises to increase its numbers. However, Montonerismo has vulnerabilities. Fragmentation within Justicialism is good. The political cannibalism exercised within Perón's party will hinder the consolidation sought by the Montonero regime. Dissidence within those ranks should be encouraged. Opposition politicians should prioritize what unites them: to stop the Marxist avalanche. Broad spectrum alliances should be coordinated.

More important than coming to power through democratic means, is to govern democratically. Plurality, today conspicuous by its absence in Argentina, can be invigorated by raising awareness of the danger in society and mobilizing in opposition to further transfers of power to the Montonero executive. In elections, reward candidates who embrace the culture of freedom, rather than statism and dependency, and use the space that remains to reclaim lost popular sovereignty. The Marxist siege has been standing. Today they are in power, but they have not yet monopolized all sectors of Argentine society. The struggle continues and can be won. The socialist dogma does not stop its advance, even in the face of the empirical wall that evidences its insane practice. May God save Argentina from such an evil experiment.

The Disappeared and War Tactics

The issue of the "disappeared" has turned out to be an ingenious and very well elaborated tool to facilitate the path to power. In the political lexicon, the act of "disappearing" someone consists of the detention and execution, without trial and unofficially, of a real or imaginary opponent. Argentina is a paradigmatic case of this phenomenon.

Unquestionably, there were disappearances in Argentina. Certainly, not the bombastic and hyperinflated numbers offered. Serious figures vary between 4,000 and 7,706. A task complicated by the constant reappearance of people considered "disappeared" and who, however, were living and active in Europe, Latin America and the former socialist countries. Subsequent compensations to relatives ensure that the numbers will never reach real proportions. The systematic practice of arresting and executing combatants without legal review was carried out by Argentine governments, both democratic and non-democratic, during the 1970s. This activity intensified with the military intervention of 1976, which lasted until 1979.

Since 1955, Argentina had already been fighting to prevent the usurpation of power by armed Marxist movements. This insurrectional force, during most of the 1960s, operated as rural guerrillas. As the public forces successfully contained the communist advance, the insurgents took the war to the cities. There began the intensification of the conflict and the conversion of it, by its symptoms, into a civil war.

Between 1969 and 1979 the communist insurgents committed 21,642 terrorist acts. Reduced, by fusion or survival, to two main groups: the People's Revolutionary Army (ERP) and the Montoneros, they became formidable urban guerrillas without renouncing the rural campaign. At that time, they were the most powerful subversive force in the continent. The Marxist premise urges, doctrinally, to violently assist the "class struggle," facilitating the extermination of all non-proletarian (read non-Marxist) classes. Argentine revolutionaries turned out to be masterful adepts, as assassinations, kidnappings, bombings, and robberies were deployed indiscriminately against trade unionists, politicians, businessmen, trade unionists, workers, executives, academics, journalists, religious, in addition to policemen, soldiers, and officers, their institutions and any family members who happened to be nearby at the time of the crime.

The Argentine public authorities, using the mechanism of capturing and unofficially killing the prisoners of the subversive forces, put an end to the war. The counteroffensive, launched by the government and the military regime in particular, neutralized the Marxists' search for power by armed means. Its members and sympathizers deserted this path and sought alternative routes to power.

The new battlefield was international public opinion. Nothing could be easier than to victimize those who lost the war. It does not matter if they were the ones who started it. The intense victimization campaign needed "victims" and "villains." Those who escaped abroad, thanks to international communism and their accomplices on the left, spectacularly choreographed the psychological onslaught.

As a methodology, it would be obligatory to decontextualize history. That way, there would be a clear "villain." They removed, from the long process of anti-subversive struggle, the period after the military coup of 1976, ignoring 21 previous years of constant warfare against the antisystem forces. This is how the trauma of the "disappeared" developed. The shameless art of decontextualizing, of making a parenthesis of only one stretch of history and pretending that it has no organic links, of making believe that all violence arose from the military coup and that they "responded" to that act, was possible only because of disinformation, aptitude towards ignorance and ideological conditioning. The effect can never be separated from the cause.

To morally judge the practice of "disappearing" is a healthy issue for a pluralistic society, as long as it is not detached from the context in which it took place. If the authorities (including the military regime of 1976) used unconventional methods to win the war, the reality is that they were not the ones who initiated them. The communist forces, particularly when they focused their war on the cities, operated entirely unconventionally. The established rules of warfare, such as wearing uniforms, targeting only uniformed personnel, and targeting locations away from the non-combatant citizenry, were intended to avoid civilian and innocent casualties.

The subversive forces, by choosing to wage their war in an unconventional manner: hiding under civilian citizenship, refusing to wear uniforms, and not operating from territories clearly marked as war zones, prescribed their future. If it is reprehensible to detain and kill an enemy combatant, it is just as reprehensible to wage war by putting at risk the lives of innocent people uninterested in "class struggle" or other doctrinal diatribes that give license for murder. The Marxist forces exercised criminal irresponsibility in the plenum of unarmed society by fighting the established order, violently, turning every street into a battlefield.

The question of whether or not all the disappeared were subversives is another point to debate. In every war, there are innocent casualties. However, no war is exempt from excesses. That includes all those who fight on both sides. The Montonero leader, Mario Firmenich, however, made notorious his insistence that most of the "disappeared" were "militants," who "with conscience, with passion" developed their actions and not innocents detached from the conspiratorial process. Besides, it is cowardice to change the title of combatants to innocent victims.

Could the military of 1976 have exercised more prudence in confronting the terrorists, since they represented the Argentine state? Would a simple police action, without any praetorian intervention, have stopped the communist offensive? Now it is improbable, if one seeks to be fair with precision, to make an analysis with decontextualized facts, far from the bloody process that aspired to the total overthrow of the social system operating since the founding of the nation, against an enemy whose soldiers were camouflaged as civilians, financed with an impressive native booty (more than $70 million at that time), plus the economic and military support of communist Cuba and the extinct USSR in the midst of the Cold War.

What is certain is that on the shoulders of the Argentine authorities at that time was the probability, or not, that the terrorists, using unconventional warfare, would seize power. Perhaps the repeal of democratic instruments, such as the Federal Criminal Court, which tried and convicted more than 2,000 subversives, and the subsequent amnesty that freed them during the 1973 war, influenced the decision. The ineffectiveness of the Cámpora and Perones governments (1973-1976) and the fact that not a single terrorist in that bloody period of the war (52% of terrorist acts were committed in those years) was convicted, may have been persuasive. One can only speculate.

The most relevant question in the issue of the "disappeared" is that of moral judgment as a tactic of war. This requires, naturally, the inclusion of the methodology of subversives. It would be unfair to pass judgment on the practice of one side and not the other. The key question then arises, in the face of a claim of victimization, what is more (or less) ethical, to detain and kill an opposing combatant, or to assassinate by placing a bomb at the bedside of an enemy? The judgment becomes more complicated and forces the inclusion of what were the purposes that gave justification to those terrible acts.

One was fighting for the defense of continuity with all its imperfections, but perfectible by evolutionary ways. The other obeyed ideas that required the destruction of all the existing order, from the most elementary, to implement an enslaving system with a lousy record. The worldwide emblematic Argentine writer of the 20th century, Jorge Luis Borges, said, "I prefer the clear sword to the furtive dynamite." I agree with Borges.

Julio M. Shiling

Of Indecents and Teachers

Considering the upheaval that Argentina is going through these days, we support freedom of expression. That is why we support the courageous attitude of the provincial governments of Neuquén and Salta. Civic protest, to preserve its valuable relevance within a functional democracy, requires a clear demarcation between what is legitimate and what is criminal. When, searching for salary increases, teachers adopt gangster attitudes by blocking roads and highways, they renounce the protection of legitimacy in any country that presumes to be a serious country. Of course, in Kirchner's Argentina, this popular disposition has become the modus operandi of those masses loyal to the current regime.

When justice is blind (or blinded) and adopts a monstrous and criminal tolerance that, with ideological prejudices, criminalizes dissident opinion and shamelessly stimulates the criminal disposition of that part of the citizenry allied to its politics, freedom is besieged. At that moment, a "right" becomes the official license to transgress. I think that the ruthless violence exercised by these anti-system groups must bring déjà vu to many of the members of Kirchner's cabinet. Longing, perhaps, for a "revolutionary" past and sympathy, no doubt, for that industry of professional "social protesters."

The death of the teacher in Neuquén is regrettable. The provincial authorities should conduct the pertinent investigations. But those responsible for the event are, in the first place, those who legitimized the irresponsible and illegal conduct that the deceased teacher was engaging in, i.e., his union. Are they teachers or political agitators? Secondly, if certain individuals decide to exceed in the application of the law, condemnable as this is, the blame will rest on the shoulders of a system incapable of maintaining order and of the central leadership that tolerates, facilitates their mobilization, pays for their operations and stimulates this "way" of protesting.

It is not a coincidence that the governors of Neuquén and Salta are not on the list of those submissive to the Kirchnerist regime. We could say that, unofficially, they have been in "disgrace" for a long time. What is certain, however, is that as long as acts of knavery are called "social protests," freedom will continue its tortuous and selective rationing. The governors of Neuquén and Salta are today fighting for the rights of Argentines to live in peace and security. All of them. Not only those who support the central government and shout the loudest, but everyone.

CHAPTER 2 VENEZUELA

Crisis in Venezuela: Barking Does Not Bring Down Tyranny

The democracies of the American continent have lost a golden opportunity to evict the Castro-Chavista regime in Caracas. The steps taken by the U.S., seconded by numerous governments of the world, recognizing Juan Guaidó as the legitimate president of Venezuela, heralded a new era of morality committed to freedom. However, everything seems to indicate that the exalted moment for the liberation of Venezuela, the last stronghold of Neo-Communism in the Americas, has already vanished.

What happened? Well, it would be better to refer to what did not happen. The old and wise saying that "foretold war does not kill soldiers" was not only violated but also flouted by the implementation of a course of deployment of verbal battalions loaded with imaginary ammunition that history has shown nourishes the will of despots to be more audacious. The truth is that, compared to the successful liberation campaigns of the past, the plan that reflected the chalkboard of the continental democracies to remove the dictator Maduro was full of inconsistencies.

The idea of approaching the Venezuelan crisis as a humanitarian issue rather than a political one was the first mistake. They put the effect before the cause. The notion of an entertainment act, a concert of good music, but in terrible taste, especially when considering the blood that has been shed in Venezuela. Even worse if we add that the organizer of the event has proven to be an admirer and friend of the Castro family. Prioritizing the humanitarian over the criminal, narcoterrorism, and the disintegration of elementary standards of civic decency was a short-sighted maneuver.

The toxicity of Latin American democratic leaders with the notion of "nonviolence" as a method to liberate countries from dictatorships under the orbit of a regime of total domination, seems, more than stupidity, a symptom of complicity. Another nonsense that has characterized this defeatist and appeasing current of the continental democratic political leadership is the position that this should and can be solved strictly among Venezuelans.

The Declaration on Venezuela recently issued by the Lima Group has been to handle the two criteria, both of which are misguided: the rejection of the use of force and a solution obtained exclusively by Venezuelans. It would seem, in the case of Venezuela, that they believe that the Cuban Castroists, the Iranians, the Russians, the Chinese, the North Koreans, the Colombians of the FARC, the ELN and the Mexicans of the drug cartels are a particular species of "Venezuelans."

Do they not remember the content of the history books and how their countries became independent or how they freed themselves from dictatorships? What makes them think that humans have improved so much that they can dispense with the use of violence while the liberticide who remains in power, precisely, does so through the monopolistic use of violence? Do they not remember how, thanks to Napoleon Bonaparte and a foreign power, half a continent gained independence from Spain? Do they know that the help of the French was crucial in gaining the freedom of Americans from the British? What to say about the Second World War!

It is time for the U.S. and the rest of the American democracies to dress up for the occasion and to stop making a big deal out of it, which only serves to falsely raise the expectations of so many people. The Venezuelans seem to have joined the list that includes the Chinese, the Vietnamese, the Kurds, the Syrians, and the Cubans (among others), who were offered war support and then shipment. May God grant that the time will come when democratic continental solidarity will be more than just recitations of documents, agreements, pacts, and letters which, in practice, are mere dead letters.

Cantinflesque Revolutions and the Eagle of the North

When historical processes begin to acquire a semblance of parody, it is time for serious reflection. When we discuss attempts to promote liberation revolutions that contain a cost of lives, of lost opportunities and end in chimeras, it is time then for a magnanimous rectification of the formula of action. Venezuela and the ongoing events are a case in point. One would think that the short gap of the 47 hours of freedom that Bolivar's homeland experienced on April 11, 2002, and which was frustrated with the despotic reinsertion of Castro-Chavismo, would have served as a lesson. It appears that the germ of the error has not been uprooted.

Where does the integral fault lie to explain the Operation Freedom fiasco? So far, the truth is complex and seems to be still hidden in the mystery of the reading given to it. Suffice it, however, to cite some follies that have risen to the surface of what happened, and which are inadmissible in the annals of defeating a ruthless enemy and liberating a country. Let's start with the Americans. The information or disinformation publicly disseminated by some high officials of the Trump administration, explaining the events that transpired, seems to belong to the screen of the cinema and of a bad movie. Here are some examples.

The U.S. Minister of State, Mike Pompeo, said that the dictator Maduro was going to board a plane to leave power, but was convinced by the Russians (they later included the Castroites) that he should stay. Elliott Abrams, the special advisor in charge of Venezuela, noted that the U.S. was in contact with high officials of the Venezuelan dictatorship and that these, at the precise moments of the action, stopped answering their cell phones. The other day in Miami, the National Security Advisor, John Bolton, offered what seemed to be the primary rationalization to explain the (tentative) economic and legal actions taken by the U.S. administration against the Cuban dictatorship. Castro's interference in Venezuela and Nicaragua were singled out as the main reason for the squeeze on Havana. This is a bit puzzling, since the reasons for wanting to see the end of communism in Cuba precede, by a long way, the coming to power of Hugo Chavez in Venezuela.

The Venezuelan organized opposition, not the popular and spontaneous mass, but the ruling elite (with rare exceptions), bears great responsibility for the disaster. The compass to indicate where the problem is and what it is made up of seems to have been lost (if they ever had it). Constant references of adherence and respect to "our constitution" is a perplexing and worrisome phenomenon. The Chavista constitution is the instrument of dictatorial legality. If they believe in it and recognize it as valid, it would be logical to conclude that either they consider themselves part of the structural machinery or they think that what exists in Venezuela is not a dictatorship. One cannot defend and insist on governing a liberation movement by the magna carta of a tyranny, call them tyrants and pretend to be morally coherent. Without a clear vision of the goal, you get nowhere. Abolish the system, or is it enough to remove Maduro?

Nonsense has abounded. Here are some examples. Interim President Juan Guaidó goes to the military base of La Carlota and insists that the gesture is and will be non-violent. This is a lousy incentive to stimulate officers to take up the weapon of pacifism, while the adversaries possess heavy military equipment and are willing to use it. Mahatma Gandhi faced a democracy. Cuban and Venezuelan communists will not extend the same courtesy to Guaidó that the British extended to the Indian pacifist. Julio Borges, former leader of the National Assembly, demonstrated gross political myopia by suggesting that, after a fall of Maduro, Venezuela could preserve relations with Russia and China. Another example is, on the one hand, the Venezuelan opposition leadership asking the people to go out and stay in the streets, but at the same time, Leopoldo López, the second visible figure in Operation Liberty, jumps from embassy to embassy looking for a comfortable protection amid a rebellion.

The worst and most outlandish of all the pronouncements and actions in this episode, worthy of a script for Cantinflas or Marty Python, has been a pronouncement by President Donald Trump. On the eve of the full implementation of the Libertad Law, no less, the U.S. president said in an interview that there could be for Castro-Communism a "new opening" if it withdraws its support for Maduro. This aberration tops all others. Let us hope that this was a verbal slip and not a moral one.

We Cubans are grateful to the nation of Lincoln for hosting us, we recognize its undeniable contribution to freedom in the world, and we generally overwhelmingly support Trump, however, we have enough memory to enumerate betrayals, embarkations and bad moves we have suffered by different administrations. Here are some of them: Kennedy (Bay of Pigs and Kennedy/Khrushchev Pact);

Johnson (suspension of secret intelligence support operatives); Nixon (Torriente Plan); Ford (Castro access to indirect trade with the U.S.); Carter (selective HR); Clinton (Title III, Helms-Burton); Bush II (not applying Title III); Obama (relations without conditions), etc.

The war of liberation against communism in our continent will continue as long as there is the will to resist and persevere, and it will see better days, with God's favor. It would come in handy if, before applying the recipe, the enemy and its nature were well understood. That would save deposits of hope, strengthen the credibility of the fighters, increase their ranks and save lives in the long run. Much can be said, for or against General Augusto Pinochet. What is indisputable is that he knew how to execute the necessary measures to free Chile from communism. May the democrats of the world take note!

CHAPTER 3 MEXICO

AMLO's Socialist Anointment

The 211th Mexican Independence Day festivities and the 6th CELAC Summit all served the purposes of elevating AMLO within the socialist ranks.

Last Thursday, September 16th, was Mexico's 211th independence declaration anniversary. A massive civic-military parade was prepared for the occasion. The event, however, was dedicated to socialism at Andres Manuel Lopez Obrador's (AMLO) request. It was not Mexico that was honored but Cuban communism. This was a pagan, political religious festival, where the command center of continental socialist imperialism, Havana, officially anointed AMLO. It was an affront to Mexico and the free world.

The Cuban dictator, Miguel Diaz-Canel, was the guest of honor. AMLO followed meticulously the script that the Marxist-Leninist government gave him. Totally denigrating himself, the Mexican head of state made embarrassing and bizarre statements all throughout the day. Communist Cuba was categorized, by him, as a "new Numantia" (a Celtiberian settlement in present-day Spain that fought Ancient Rome). AMLO added, "I think that it should be declared a World Heritage site for the same reason." The Castro regime's primary survivability focus, having the U.S. end the embargo, was a predictable chore that Mexico's president would take up for the Castro-Communist dictatorship.

Functioning in customary lackey fashion, AMLO directed the Castro regime's message to, both, the American government and the Cuban exile community. For the Biden-Harris administration, the communication was predictable: "lift the blockade (a misnomer: it is actually an embargo)." To Cubans living free in the U.S., the Mexican president called on them to, in effect, end the fight for freedom, forgo their brethren's natural rights on the Island to live freely and accept the communist dictatorship as an immutable fact.

Castro-Communism, since it took power in 1959, immediately began its war to impose socialism in the Americas. For a thirty-year period, the Soviet Union foot the bill and Cuba was the material agent of subversion. Since the collapse of the USSR, dictator Fidel Castro concocted the Sao Paulo Forum (SPF) in 1990 to continue the Marxist-Leninist siege, but with a reformulated methodology, since the Soviet subventions had dried out. Venezuela was the first country to adopt this new dictatorial prototype. With Havana giving the orders and Chavez's puppet regime draining Venezuela's wealth to the finance this war, socialism made more advancements in the thirty years following the SPF communist reconfiguration strategy, than in the same preceding timeframe.

Communist Cuba is anxious to give AMLO a bigger role in this socialist hegemonic campaign. The Mexican president is a natural for this job for many reasons. As a true believer in socialism, this ideologue, who has transitioned from the Institutional Revolutionary Party (PRI) to the Party of the Democratic Revolution (PRD) and finally, in 2018, to the National Regeneration Movement (Morena), has always enjoyed Havana's support and is a dependable radical. Some in intelligence circles, have suggested that AMLO's founding of Morena was crafted on the Cuban regime's advice. There are many reasons why the Mexican president is much revered by Castroism.

The tacit acquiescence AMLO has with his country's drug cartels, given the importance of drug trafficking funds for promoting and sustaining continental socialism, is a clear asset. Mexico has the second largest economy in Latin America (after Brazil), where the U.S. is its biggest trading partner. The enormous border it shares with America and its function as a de facto border guard for Washington, gives Mexico great leverage. Castro-Communism knows all this very well and feels the time has come to make greater use of AMLO.

The Community of Latin American and Caribbean States (CELAC) is another Castroite SPF invention, which Hugo Chávez unveiled in 2010. Its purpose is to demerit the Organization of American States and challenge U.S. influence in the region. The latest gathering for the CELAC, its 6th summit, was hosted by AMLO in Mexico on Saturday September 18th and attended by more than a dozen presidents and prime ministers. "We should build in the American continent," said the Mexican president, "something similar to what was the economic community that was the beginning of the current European Union." AMLO speaking for leftism, has no intention of opening democratic spaces. To the contrary.

The socialist continental project does not seek to limit political activism to Latin American actors. This 6th CELAC Summit provided evidence of who the left wants to partner with. At AMLO's request, the Chinese dictator, Xi Jinping, by way of a video, addressed the event. China's tyrannical ruler said "China-Latin America relations have entered a new era featuring equality, mutual benefit, innovation, openness and tangible benefits for the people."

Despite courageous pronunciations against the communist regimes of Cuba, Venezuela, and Nicaragua by the presidents of Uruguay and Paraguay, Luis Lacalle Pou and Mario Abdo Benítez, respectively, the CELAC is structurally and morally irreformable. All democratic leaders should follow the example of Brazil's president, Jair Bolsonaro, who withdraw his country from the organization citing, most correctly, its bias towards leftist dictatorships. During the summit, Nicolas Maduro called for a permanent CELAC headquarters to be erected in Mexico. The Venezuelan dictator knows of Havana's intention of making AMLO a more prominent figure in this socialist hemispheric onslaught.

The 211th Mexican Independence Day festivities and the 6th CELAC Summit, all served the purposes of elevating AMLO within the socialist ranks. This is why Communist Cuba, the grandmaster of Marxist-Leninist subversion in the Western Hemisphere, was the privileged guest of honor. Ironically, that very Thursday, September 16th, the European Parliament voted overwhelmingly to condemn the Castro regime for its gross conduct in the aftermath of the Cuban Uprising of July 11th. Additionally, the EU political body sanctioned individuals and institutions responsible for the heinous acts, under the "Magnitsky Law." This was a brutal defeat for Cuban communism and its apologists like AMLO. It is now obvious that Mexico is clearly in the Castro regime's plan for a socialist offensive. Biden-Harris cannot be counted on for anything that deals with combating socialism. Havana, Beijing, and Tehran know this also.

CHAPTER 4 BOLIVIA

Towards a Model of Democratic Rescue: Lessons From Bolivia

Communists and their associates aside, the liberation of Bolivia has given much reason to celebrate. Not only for the happiness of seeing how the citizens of this landlocked anomalous land confronted one of the tyrannies of continental socialism and won, but also because they prevented Castro-Communism from rescuing one of its satellites. Such are destinies. Bolivia, we cannot forget, has the historical privilege of being the place where the assassin Che Guevara was executed.

The most relevant steps to follow to ensure that the freedom achieved in the Andean country is not reversed is to establish order, preventing subversive forces loyal to the dictator Morales from trying to destabilize the liberation process, dismantle all dictatorial institutions and apply justice with transparency, finality, and comprehensively. Bolivia was not ruled by an autochthonous or independent tyrant, but by a system: international communism, directed from Havana, reformulated since 1990 after the fall of the USSR with the Sao Paulo Forum (SPF), containing a new methodological dictatorial model (SPF model). The criminal regime of Morales was a result of that prototype.

When we speak of the SPF model as a practical scheme, we refer to a paradigm that is composed of a Leninist State guided from communist Cuba, a pragmatic ideological attachment to communism/socialism and a hybrid mercantilist economy that includes as part of its strategic programming: (1) the adulteration of the Constitution, "reforming" it with a dictatorial constituent; (2) having votes, controlling the electoral body responsible for counting the votes; (3) a loyal and appeasing opposition; (4) destroying or co-opting the Armed Forces. AA; (5) neutralizing the judicial branch; (6) selective/limited freedom of the press; (7) absorbing the business class; (8) attempting to penetrate organized religion; and (9) developing a simulacrum of a civil society with pro-government front organizations.

This whole new structural mechanism of promoting communism in the 21st century has benefited from the current intellectual framework, postmodernism, that project of cultural Marxism that presents diverse fronts including political ecology, gender ideology, multiculturalism, radical feminism, mass immigration, citizen disarmament, etc.

The SPF model has managed to control political power in Venezuela (Chavismo 1998), Brazil (Lula-Dilma 2002, 2010), Argentina (Kirchnerism 2003, 2019), Uruguay (Frente Amplio 2004, 2009), Dominican Republic (PLD/PRD 1996, 2004, 2008), Bolivia (Morales 2005), Chile (Bachelet 2006, 2014), Ecuador (Correa 2006), Nicaragua (Sandinismo 2006), Honduras (Zelaya 2006), Paraguay (Lugo 2008), El Salvador (FMLN 2009, 2014), Panama (PRD 2009, 2019), Peru (Humala 2011) and Mexico (AMLO 2018). There have also been numerous subversive movements/parties attempting to achieve power throughout the continent with adherence to this Marxist bloc, most notably the FARC and ELN of Colombia.

Not all of them, however, have been successful in implementing this neo-Marxist prototype to the full. Why has the dictatorial model of the SPF been successfully implemented in some countries where they have governed and not in others? The answer lies in the condition of the most seminal variables of the paradigm. In Venezuela, Nicaragua, Ecuador (until Moreno arrived) and Bolivia (until recently) the political pattern has been successfully implemented. In Honduras and Paraguay, precocious dictators were institutionally removed: one by the public forces and the other by an impeachment trial. Brazil, a symbolic cradle of the SPF model where Lula da Silva and the PT served as a logistical bastion for the invention of the tyrant Fidel Castro, did not manage to consolidate the post-Soviet communist despotic model. Why?

In the successful case of Brazil, that of Bolivia recently, where a base of Castro-Communism was established without much difficulty, and the examples of Venezuela and Nicaragua, regrettable cases whose heroic deeds of liberation have failed, the answer stands out. Of the nine variables of the SPF model previously mentioned, the most determinant for the insertion and preservation of the Castro-Communist prototype of the 21st century is the co-optation of the Armed Forces and the formulation of a manipulable opposition/dissidence attentive to follow the dictates of the Leninist principle of peaceful coexistence, which always invokes "dialogue" as a mechanism of dictatorial survival. Let us look at the facts.

In Venezuela and Nicaragua there were massive demonstrations, for extended periods of time, throughout each country respectively. Paralyzing the nations of

Bolivar and Dario. In both cases, the Armed Forces remained in line with the tyrannies, assaulted the civilian population and committed crimes against humanity. In short, they propped up the tyrannical status quo. In both examples, too, there was an opposition/dissidence always willing to follow the suicidal course of "dialogue" with the executioner.

Brazil, despite the efforts of Lula da Silva and Dilma Rousseff to penetrate and corrupt the Armed Forces, never succeeded. The opposition in Brazil was always combative and never made any pact with the Castro-Communist bloc. An examination of the other countries where the proles of the SPF governed, but failed in rooting their despotic model, reveals that in most cases the Armed Forces remained impenetrable (Dominican Republic, Chile, Paraguay, Honduras, El Salvador, Uruguay, Peru).

The brave Bolivian people defied the dictator Morales and managed to break away from the Castro-Communist empire. Faced with the tyrannical acts of the coca grower oppressor, Bolivian society exercised the sacrosanct principle of the right to rebellion. This act, consistent with democratic values and incorporated into the most dignified political proclamations, also corresponds to the military.

Another thing: the relevant Bolivian opposition rejected any understanding with the dictatorship.

Democracy is not a matter of mere procedures. Even less so when they are fraudulent. Democracy has much more to do with values such as freedom and all that is necessary to protect it. A "coup" is carried out when the basic precepts that sustain democracy are swept away, not when the homeland is rescued. The communists' tantrum over the loss of a colony should not move the free world. On the contrary. Bolivia offers us a model of action to liberate captive nations.

CHAPTER 5 CHILE

Schumpeter and Lesson's From Chile's Debacle

Joseph Schumpeter may well help us better understand the debacle that was Chile's 2021 presidential election result of Sunday, December 19. Far-left candidate Gabriel Boric easily won with 55.87% of the vote, defeating conservative Jose Antonio Kast, a staunch defender of free markets and republican governance. How could arguably Latin America's basket case of success in the late 20th and early 21st centuries, measured by socio-economic indicators, have gone for a Marxist sympathizer?

The Austrian economist and politician (Schumpeter) authored a classic, *Capitalism, Socialism, and Democracy* (1942), where he contended that socialism would ultimately overrun capitalism and democracy. The rationale Schumpeter offered was that as political equality extended voting rights, the non-wealthy portion of the population, clearly the majority, would vote for socialism. The Moravian-born, later naturalized U.S. citizen, and former Harvard professor was most influential in the field of economics. Yet, his 1942 work may prove to be

Schumpeter's biggest legacy. In this pessimistic work, his understanding of human nature is playing out.

Chile is not an isolated case. Peru and Honduras are recent examples where socialist candidates won the presidency. Elections scheduled for 2022 in Brazil, Colombia, and Costa Rica, place these countries all within plausible reach by radical leftism. The failure of socialism is undeniable when judged by empirical evidence and moral history. Yet, despite this fact, how can socialism's appeal at the voting booth be explained?

The right, that political smorgasbord comprised of liberals, libertarians, conservatives, Christian Democrats, and a convoluted mixture of all these different parts, has not been a good salesperson. The left, on the other hand, has been formidable in selling itself. Does anyone doubt this? As a system, socialism, irrefutably, has caused 100 to 130 million deaths in the 20th century. Its premier and original economic model have been forced to undergo major overhauls to avoid famines (China, Vietnam, etc.). Its epistemological base—classical Marxism—has been disproven by history as early as World War I. The fact that this malevolent system still has an attractiveness to large portions of people is proof that the Left has better convincing skills.

Sebastián Piñera (Chile), Mauricio Macri (Argentina), Juan Manuel Santos and Iván Duque (Colombia) are all examples of Latin American RINOs (Republicans in Name Only). The U.S. has its own group of these politicians that are accredited logistically with the Republican Party but not morally or philosophically. Piñera paved the way for the Marxist agitator who won the presidency in Chile, by legitimizing the subversive war that the International Left waged on Chilean democracy. It was his support of institutional mechanisms to dismantle the republic, like the referendum, that laid the groundwork for the socialist revolutionaries to dig deep and insist on a systemic overthrow. Piñera surrendered Chile to the Marxists a while back. Similar defeats can be pointed to in Macri's Argentina, and Santos' and Duque's Colombia.

As Marxists took to culture to focus their heaviest artillery, the 5 institutions Antonio Gramsci identified as vital to defeat free societies, the family, religion, media, education, and law, are all under attack and the last 3 have become virtual fiefdoms of leftism. When one adds to this challenging reality, postmodernism's relativization of truth and knowledge, the task of socialist proselytizing has been made easy.

The civic revolt one is witnessing in the U.S. by the Right (liberals, libertarians, conservatives, Christian Democrats) against Marxist policies and socialist politicians is what is needed in Latin America. Ideology matters! Freedom, family, free enterprise, God, country and a vibrant middle class are much more reasonably conducive factors to personal and spiritual empowerment, as well as material prosperity. Schumpeter's dismal forecast need not be played out. That huge mass of individuals that can fit into that block of the "Right," must appeal to people's emotions, not just their intellect. The Left must be defeated in their own game.

CHAPTER 6 COLOMBIA

Gustavo Petro: Castro-Communism's Manchurian Candidate

The SPF dictatorial paradigm haunts Colombia. Petro is Havana's man in the 2022 presidential election.

Colombia will soon have presidential elections. Its stable democracy, despite nearly 62 non-consecutive years of political violence instigated primarily by left-wing subversive groups (1948-1958, 1964-2016), may be facing its biggest threat. Gustavo Petro, the front-runner in Colombia's presidential race, is a wholly fabricated product of Castro-Communism. Petro is socialism's Manchurian candidate.

Communism's appetite in the Americas goes back to the founding of the Soviet Union. In Colombia, the most successful Marxist operation was the *Bogotazo*. At the 9th Pan-American Conference held on April 9, 1948, there was international communism's first aggressive attempt of assaulting power in the South American country. The assassination of presidential candidate Jorge Eliécer Gaitán triggered massive riots that sprung from Soviet-contrived disinformation. Among those present on that "Black

Friday" were Cuban communists Fidel Castro and Rafael del Pino.

Communist Cuba became a Soviet-launching pad from the onset. In 1959, Castro-Communism begin a targeted subversive campaign of immersing itself in the affairs of every single country in the Americas. Of particular interest to the Castro regime were Argentina, Colombia, and Venezuela. In the Colombian case, the three main Marxist terrorist organizations that were formed with Cuban assistance were the National Liberation Army (ELN) (1964), Colombian Revolutionary Armed Forces (FARC) (1964), and the 19th of April Movement (M-19) (1970s).

The ELN and M-19 were structurally formulated in Havana. As long as the Soviet subsidies poured into the island, violent revolutions were the norm. The fall of the USSR changed all that. No longer able to finance the costs of communist insurgencies, the acquisition of political power by armed aggression had to be reinvented. The Marxist regime in Havana sought new avenues to power for Latin America, at the Sao Paulo Forum (SPF) in 1990.

A new dictatorial model was contrived by Cuban tyrant Fidel Castro and his protégé, Lula de Silva. The SPF prototype dictated that power be acquired by making use of democracy. The rule was to compete in elections, subvert the democratic institutions after having won, and then deconstruct republican systems. Venezuela, Ecuador, Nicaragua, and Bolivia were initial success stories of the SPF model.

The deceased Cuban dictator put enormous pressure on all three Colombian communist guerrillas to adopt the new, post-Soviet socialist strategy designed in 1990. The M-19 was the first to abide by Castro's instructions. Slowly, the ELN followed suit. The FARC proved more hesitant. The lucrative drug business, along with the lax policies of presidents César Gaviria, Ernesto Samper, and Andrés Pastrana, undoubtedly contributed to this. The 2002 ascendancy of Álvaro Uribe changed the dynamics. By waging war to defeat the FARC and pacify Colombia, Uribe achieved what he sought.

Gustavo Petro joined M-19 at the age of 17. Thoroughly trained as a terrorist, Petro quickly put into practice Castro's plan. At the Cuban tyrant's request, about 1990 Petro changed the guerrilla uniform for the disguise of a "democrat." In 1991, Petro began his rise through different branches and positions in Colombian politics. Cleverly, masquerading as a social democrat, he remains a structured socialist.

Castroism's journey, to institute the radical Marxist guerrillas into Colombian politics, officially began with a 1993 state visit by the Cuban despot to Colombia. By 2012, with the Colombian government's military victory over the FARC subversives, the Castro regime, supported by Pope Francis' Vatican, and the Obama administration, began a "peace" agreement scheme. Four years of negotiation sought to grant immunity from prosecution to the Colombian terrorist group for the war crimes and crimes against humanity that it had been committing since 1964. Understanding that a new administration in Bogotá, under the leadership of Juan Manuel Santos, stood a greater chance of securing such an agreement, it was put to the test of a popular referendum.

The "peace" agreement orchestrated by Cuban communism was rejected by the Colombian people on October 2, 2016. Notwithstanding the will and the principle of popular sovereignty, Santos overrode the Colombian people's wish, "revised" the agreement and maneuvered through Congress to get its approval. The Castro regime's plan to incorporate the FARC into the Colombian political landscape was finally achieved.

Petro has played the part in strict accordance with the Cuban dictatorship's playbook. The former M-19 terrorist (Petro) has successfully masqueraded his candidacy as one of the "center-left." The existence of FARC-supported politicians lends itself to this deceit. Havana has been the architect of all the riots which have plagued the Duque presidency. There is an incredible tactical similarity between the subversive activity prevalent in Colombian and Chilean cities (before Boric). The SPF dictatorial paradigm haunts Colombia. Petro is Havana's man in the 2022 presidential election.

CHAPTER 7 PERU

Socialism Loses and Freedom Wins in Peru

The Sao Paulo Forum (SPF) dictatorial offensive, designed by communist Cuba to spread socialism throughout Latin America, suffered a big setback on Wednesday, December 7 in Peru. President Pedro Castillo attempted a coup by ordering the dissolution of Congress, initiating the installment of an "emergency" government, ordered a national curfew, and called for the revamping of the country's democratic constitution. In its place, predictably, it would be substituted with socialist legalism. The forces of freedom saved the day for Peru and potentially for the Americas.

The Peruvian congress acted swiftly after Castillo wanted to bypass an incipient congressional motion that sought to constitutionally displace him from the presidency. By a 101 to 29 clear majority vote, the legislative body reverted the Marxist former president's Bolshevik-style power grab. Additionally, the mistake made by Bolivian authorities during its 2019 liberation process was not repeated in Peru.

Castillo was quickly arrested and now faces criminal charges under the Peruvian Penal Code's Title XVI in

Chapter 1 and Article 346. Acting smart and with civic determination, Peru's legitimate public forces closed off passages to the embassies of socialist dictatorial regimes like Bolivia's. The urgency with which the Peruvian Congress acted, and the complimentary measures taken to safeguard democracy, should serve as a model to challenge the SPF dictatorial model.

Colombia's Gustavo Petro, Brazil's Lula da Silva, Chile's Gabriel Boric, Mexico's Manuel López Obrador, and Argentina's Alberto and Cristina Fernández, undoubtedly, must be in shock mode. After all, it was the SPF playbook of winning elections, proceeding to dismantle (or attempt to) democratic institutions, destroy the separation of powers, stamping out the constitution, and tolerating a sterile opposition was what provided them with a path to power. Venezuela, Nicaragua, Bolivia, and Cuba, the master planner, potentially, could lose momentum and continue to suffer reversions.

This is the moment for the U.S. to build a coalition of Western democracies and insist that the rule of law be followed. This means that Castillo and his co-plotters be held accountable. Furthermore, the diplomatic corps (intelligence operation bases) of Latin America's, Russia, and China's non-democratic regimes that have supported the coup instigators should be carefully monitored. This is not the moment for unprincipled debates, which surely the Castro-Communist regime will push for to buy time in its attempt to save the SPF's project in this Andean nation. Peru is today an inspiration of liberty. Its bold action should be emulated.

CHAPTER 8 INTERFERENCE, SUMMITS AND DEMOCRACY

Is Russia Plotting a War Front in Latin America?

The Cuban, Venezuelan, and Nicaraguan dictatorships are probably more concerned than Washington and Brussels over the Kremlin's diatribes.

The Soviet Union's understanding of doctrinal internationalism split the world into regional spheres of influence, but with a caveat. The popular adage of the Brezhnev Doctrine's "what's mine is mine and what's yours is up for grabs" principle, was the cornerstone of Soviet foreign policy. It has been carried forward by the post-Soviet authoritarian regime of Vladimir Putin. Russia's blatant disregard for Ukrainian sovereignty and the civilized order of political relations is evidence of this. Recent declarations by high-ranking American military leaders and State Department officials have issued stark security warnings. Could Russia be plotting a Latin American, Ukraine-like, war front?

During a Senate Foreign Affairs Committee hearing on March 31, Deputy Assistant Secretary for Public

Diplomacy, Policy, Planning, and Coordination, Kerri Hannan, testified about Russia's threat in the Western Hemisphere. "The commitment to democracy in the Hemisphere has never seemed so urgent," Hannan stated and added that "while Russia tramples on Ukraine's democracy and threatens to export the Ukrainian crisis to the Americas, expanding its military cooperation with Cuba, Nicaragua and Venezuela." GOP Senator Marco Rubio (FL) concurred with the State Department official and said, "Russia is an acute problem, and it is a current challenge."

Hannan's testimonial declaration is not an isolated assessment. General Laura J. Richardson, the commander of the U.S. Southern Command, raised similar concerns on March 8 over Russian collusion with Latin American socialist dictatorships. Before members of the House Armed Services Committee, Richardson said that "Threats in South America, include transnational criminal organization as well as the meddling of both China and Russia." The four-star general highlighted to Congress that "Russia, a more immediate threat, is increasing its engagements in the hemisphere."

Yury Borisov, the Kremlin's deputy prime minister, said in January that he could "neither affirm nor exclude" whether Russia would send military assets to Cuba or Venezuela. It is worth noting that days before the Russian invasion of Ukraine, Borisov paid a visit to Cuba, Venezuela, and Nicaragua. Dictator Putin has developed a close relationship with the tyrannical troika of Miguel Díaz-Canel, Nicolás Maduro, and Daniel Ortega. Russian state news agencies have made no secret of this alliance. Russian Foreign Minister Sergey Lavrov said in an address to the State Duma (Russia's figurative parliament) in January that "the three friendly countries agreed to consider ways to further deepen our strategic partnership in each and every field."

Putin's top diplomat simply stated an obvious fact. Except for an 8-year hiatus (1991-1999), Russia has maintained a tight bond with Latin American socialism. The former KGB officer, undoubtedly, revamped the post-totalitarian model from which he came. The mixture of a crony and state capitalist-driven economy, Putinism shares many key characteristics with the Sao Paulo Forum's dictatorial prototype, that concocted scheme devised by the deceased Cuban tyrant, Fidel Castro, in reaction to the fall of Soviet communism.

The Soviet Union invested heavily in promoting communism in the Americas. Putin's willingness to forgive $53 billion of Russian debt owed by the Castro-Communist dictatorship, reflects the understanding of a partnered relationship. Russia's activism in Latin America, following in the USSR's footsteps, is channeled through Castro's Cuba. The Russian GPS satellite spy base on the outskirts of Managua, the expansive military hardware transfer to Venezuela, and the espionage experimentation that, most likely, resulted in the Havana Syndrome in Cuba, all predate the invasion of Ukraine.

Putin may be seeking to scare the U.S.; threats of bringing the Russo-Ukrainian War into America's backyard could shed, however, surprising consequences for his regime, as well as Cuba, Venezuela, and Nicaragua. The people in those three captive nations could emulate the Ukrainians. A revolt is a possibility. If the Russian dictator arms and uses Cuban, Venezuelan, and Nicaraguan territory, they would be considered complicit war allies, like Belarus.

Such a scenario would prompt the West to extend sanctions against the three socialist regimes. Given the mixing of geography and national security, the U.S. and NATO would likely send war vessels to the Gulf of Mexico, the

Florida Straits, and the Caribbean Sea. Putin has proved to be a bumbling war strategist. The Cuban, Venezuelan, and Nicaraguan dictatorships are probably more concerned than Washington and Brussels over the Kremlin's diatribes. Ukraine may well be a key to freedom in Latin America.

Biden's Americas Summit Opportunity

Will Biden stand his ground, or will he give in to socialist regimes and invite tyrants and human rights violators to the Summit of the Americas?

The Biden administration has a great opportunity to emphasize that democracy is the gold standard political system in the Western Hemisphere. The 9th Summit of the Americas, which is to be held the week of June 6-10 in Los Angeles, California, was poised to exclude most of the continent's non-democratic regimes. Certain Latin American leaders objected to the prohibition of the dictatorships in Cuba, Venezuela, and Nicaragua from the event and stated that they would boycott the conference if this occurred. The overarching dilemma for Biden is whether he will placate the left and invite these notorious human rights violators or will the U.S. firmly defend stated principles that bind hemispheric cordiality based on the practice of consensual modes of governance and free societies.

U.S. Assistant Secretary of State Brian A. Nichols stated during a television program on May 2 that "Cuba, Nicaragua, [and] the Maduro regime do not respect the Inter-American Democratic Charter, and therefore I don't expect their presence." When questioned on the specific case of Cuba, where during the 2015 Summit the Cuban dictator, Raul Castro, was invited, Nichols commented that, while it will ultimately be Biden's prerogative, he believes "the president has been very clear about the presence of countries that by their actions do not respect democracy — they will not receive invitations."

Jen Psaki on May 10 questioned the firmness of Nichols' statement. During a White House briefing, the president's press secretary said that "no invitations have been issued at this point." What Biden's media representative was suggesting, was that the Summit's door was still open to hemispheric dictatorships. The White House's apparent about-face reflects a reaction to the Mexican president's affirmation that if the three autocratic regimes were excluded, he would boycott the event.

Andrés Manuel López Obrador took this public stance, coincidently after having just concluded an official visit to communist Cuba. On the imprisoned island, he met with Cuban dictators Raúl Castro and Miguel Díaz-Canel. In addition to the usual diatribe against the American embargo on the Castro-Communist regime and other victimization follies, the Mexican president was awarded a dictatorial-sponsored medal. It is interesting to note that this same "distinction" has been bestowed upon Saddam Hussein, Vladimir Putin, Hugo Chávez, Daniel Ortega, Nicolás Maduro, Nicolae Ceauşescu, Muammar Gaddafi, Evo Morales, Erich Honecker, Viktor Yanukovych, and Xi Jinping, among others. All have been serial offenders of gross human rights violations. AMLO, a staunch collaborator of continental socialism, followed the script he received from Havana well.

Luís Arce, Bolivia's figurative president, announced on Wednesday, May 11, that he will also boycott next month's Summit if the three socialist dictatorships are not invited. It is worthy to point out that the Bolivian regime should also have been on Biden's list of countries to exclude. Evo Morales has instituted the Sao Paulo Forum dictatorial prototype in this land-locked country. Its rigged elections, persecution of political opponents, and the absence of the rule of law annul any democratic credentials.

The Russian invasion of Ukraine has highlighted many things. Two important factors stand out. The U.N. has proved to be worth little in solving seminal problems. This is because dictatorships sit alongside democracies and false equivalents are established. This moral inequality only serves tyranny. Organizations structured along with certain qualitative criteria, like NATO, for example, have offered a contrasting value. The Summit of the Americas was conceived, since its first meeting in Miami, Florida, in 1994, tightly linked to the democratic system of government. Its parent entity, the Organization of American States (OAS), was wholly founded on the premise that democracy was to be its exclusive model of sociopolitical exercise.

The OAS's foundational charter preceded the U.N.'s Universal Human Rights Declaration by over seven months. In other words, many aspects of the OAS' inherent principles were adopted in the U.N. document. Signed in Bogotá, Colombia on April 30, 1948, and amended in 1967, 1985, 1992, 1993, and 1997, the overriding innateness of the organism was freedom, liberal democracy, and representative governments. Its preamble states the belief "that the true significance of American solidarity and good neighborliness can only mean the consolidation on this continent, within the framework of democratic institutions, of a system of individual liberty and social justice based on respect for the essential rights of man." It adds as one of its objectives, "to promote and consolidate representative democracy," (Art.1, Sec. B). It heightens that "the solidarity of the American States and the high aims which are sought through it require the political organization of those States on the basis of the effective exercise of representative democracy," (Art. 3, Sec. D). Let's hope Biden upholds the Summit's reason to be.

Is Democracy the Gold Standard System for the Americas?

The overarching dilemma here is how can a free republic expose itself to annihilation by allowing an antisystem candidate like Petro to compete for power?

When we refer to an area such as the Americas, does geography or a set of values have primacy? An argument can be made for both. Systems of government, however, have increasingly become the primary measure in classifying what binds nations, rather than where they are located on the map. The Americas, as judged by regional accords and practicing doctrines, aligned itself in the modern era with the second factor. The Western Hemisphere made it known, following World War I, that democracy and free societies would be the accepted norm of governance and societal arrangement.

Europe made this clear when World War II concluded, and the Cold War began. East and West became, not geographic boundaries, but determinants of freedom and totalitarian socialism. Suddenly, being part of the West included countries in the East such as Japan, South Korea, Australia, Taiwan, just to name a few. Western civilization, that fusion of Jerusalem, Athens, and Rome, incorporated non-Christian nations. Values became the guiding rule.

When we refer to an area such as the Americas, does geography or a set of values have primacy? An argument can be made for both. Systems of government, however, have increasingly become the primary measure in classifying what binds nations, rather than where they are located on the map. The Americas, as judged by regional accords and practicing doctrines, aligned itself in the modern era with the second factor. The Western Hemisphere made it known, following World War I, that democracy and free societies would be the accepted norm of governance and societal arrangement.

Europe made this clear when World War II concluded, and the Cold War began. East and West became, not geographic boundaries, but determinants of freedom and totalitarian socialism. Suddenly, being part of the West included countries in the East such as Japan, South Korea, Australia, Taiwan, just to name a few. Western civilization, that fusion of Jerusalem, Athens, and Rome, incorporated non-Christian nations. Values became the guiding rule.

The Western Hemisphere has always fallen more within a context of North/South, where the divide were systems of wealth production and distribution and transparency in politics. This has not been accidentally or by chance. The Left in Latin America has crafted a clever idiomatic approach to class warfare strategies. Putting aside linguistic and cultural differences between Anglos and Hispanics (or Latins), the structural formation of regional consolidation was intended to rest on the principle of consensual government. That meant a hemispheric belief that a republican system that exercised democracy was the continent's choice.

Numerous political documents were drafted that specified that to be the case. The foundational Charter of the Organization of American States (OAS) (1948), the San José Charter (1969), the Viña del Mar Declaration (1996), the Quebec Declaration (2001), and the Inter-American Democratic Charter (2001) are some of the American affirmations that emphasize that democracy and representative governments are the established norm of political operation in the Western Hemisphere.

Despite this clear commitment to guide state policy across the continent, dictatorships have continually pestered the region. Some, like the Castro-Communist have lasted for over six decades and the Chavez-Castroist for more than two. In dealing with this contrast between theory and practice, there have been two historical and competing doctrines that have been followed. One is the Estrada Doctrine (1930), named after Mexican Secretary of Foreign Affairs, Genaro Estrada. This served as the intellectual instrument of praxis that embraced the premise of non-intervention in other countries affairs, accepting non-democratic regimes as legitimate based on their de facto control of power. The Estrada Doctrine delighted dictatorships as geography legitimized political rule, rather than governments that honor human rights.

The competing instrument was morally compelling and agreeing with the OAS purpose of supporting free societies. The Betancourt Doctrine (1959), named after Venezuelan president Romulo Betancourt, established an ethical code of conduct for the governments of the Americas to follow. It supported the position that dictatorships, whether they come from an ideological framework of the Left or the Right, not be recognized or welcomed into the regional community of free republics. Additionally, the Betancourt Doctrine advocated proactive state measures, overt and covert, to help liberate captive nations in the Western Hemisphere. This signified a democratic ethos at its finest.

Today, Cuba, Venezuela, Nicaragua, and Bolivia are clear dictatorships. Chile and Peru are on course to become non-democratic regimes, following the scripted Sao Paulo Forum dictatorial prototype (1990). Argentina and Mexico are run by governments there are part of the socialist axis of continental despotism, directed by the Castro regime. This Sunday, June 19, Columbia will hold a seminal presidential election. An unfavorable result could tip the scale and leave the American principle of democratic governance in a weakened minority position.

The Marxist candidate, Gustavo Petro should lose the election to the outsider, Rodolfo Hernandez. Fortunately, Colombia has a majority electoral system, which requires a second round, in the absence of an absolute majority. Had there been in place a plurality election model, Colombia would be on its way to communist consolidation. This is how Chile's Salvador Allende and Nicaragua's Daniel Ortega reached power (for Ortega it was the second time). The overarching dilemma here is how can a free republic expose itself to annihilation by allowing an antisystem candidate like Petro to compete for power?

This is a question that the great republican continental leaders that formulated democracy and the values that flow from this exercise of governance as the Americas' norm, failed to address. Democratic elections were never designed to facilitate the ascension of power to autocrats. It is time for an effective Plan B to be drawn. Perhaps a beefed-up Betancourt Doctrine needs to surface. Smart electoral systems could also help.

CHAPTER 9 SAO PAULO FORUM

Sao Paulo Forum: The Castro-Communist International

The Soviet Union (USSR) did not invent communism, but it was the first modern state to successfully implement this system. The version of socialism/communism that survived the war between the factions of the 19th century internationals was the pseudo-scientific one concocted by Karl Marx and Friedrich Engels.

Epistemologically, this was an assemblage composed of fragments of German philosophy (Hegel, Feuerbach), English political economy (Locke, Smith, Ricardo), French socialism (Babeuf, Fourier, Saint-Simon, Proudhon, Rousseau) and all this content lay within a positivist abode (Comte) that, consequently, would employ an economic coordination faithful to socialist precepts (centralized, planning, productive/distributive means in governmental hands).

It fell to Vladimir Lenin and the Bolsheviks to give a blatant coup d'état to the incipient Russian democracy to mold the ideas of Marx and Engels into a political project. Irremediably, the praxis of this experiment conditioned its feasibility to the structuring of society and political power within the parameters of a regime of total domination. It is true that there were modifications of this pattern and exercises of practical and ideological pragmatism to monopolize survival. The goal of universalizing communist hegemony, however, remained an unchanging obsession throughout the 20th century.

The tool of recruitment and penetration to promote the imperialist project of communism was the sequence of "internationals" and screen organizations that the USSR forged and sponsored to agglutinate and direct all Marxist-Leninist movements and regimes in the world. First it was the Comintern (III International 1919-1943), then the Cominform (1947-1956) and finally forged institutions such as the CAME, the Warsaw Pact and a large group of disguised organizations all over the world, all under the tutelage of Moscow and together with the KGB and the Soviet politburo. In addition, the USSR trained, financed, and supported the expansion of international communism, directly and indirectly, by arms with proactive satellites such as the Popular Front (Spain), Communist Cuba, Islamic groups and Marxist-Leninist movements entitled "anti-colonizers," "national liberation," pseudo-religious "Third World" and liberation theology, etc. Undoubtedly, this ambitious project of socialist enlargement and sustenance came at an extraordinary cost.

When the U.S. reformulated its policy to combat the communist offensive from one of containment (Truman Doctrine) to one of reversal (Reagan Doctrine), the dynamics changed in favor of the democratic order. The inadequacy of the USSR's productive capacity to deal with the galloping cost of maintaining and promoting the global Marxist empire and to face the new challenge of the U.S. forced modifications to its operational model in an attempt at survival that was not achieved. The idea of transforming the economic format without altering the Leninist state, as the Chinese and Vietnamese did successfully, was not received with enthusiasm by the Soviet bureaucrats. Mikhail Gorbachev, the man put there by the politburo to save communism, not finding the support to modify the economy, amended the political environment in the hope of finding support for the economic reforms he was looking for. In the attempt, by sterilizing the most fundamental pillar of totalitarian control of political power, democratic centralism, it got out of hand and Soviet communism collapsed.

The collapse of the Berlin Wall and the dissolution of the USSR two years later did not mean the fall of communism. What vanished was only the methodological and hegemonic Soviet version. Communism mutated. The Cuban dictator Fidel Castro was the architect and intellectual author of the rescue of international communism from then on. He chose as his sponsoring partner Luis Ignacio Lula da Silva, a communist trade unionist with good relations with Castro's intelligence. The Brazilian Marxist's native country was a convenient calculation. Brazil offered many benefits, serving as a stage from which a new strategic project could be launched to save and relaunch communism. In addition to being the most populous nation in Latin America, an economic powerhouse and bordering ten countries in South America, Brazil presented a "non-aligned" or "Third World" face and Lula's Marxist-leaning Workers Party had experience navigating the political process within a democracy. What better place to organize a communist renewal international than Sao Paulo?

Since its founding in 1990, the Sao Paulo Forum (SPF), a metaphysical and structural imitation of internationals such as the Comintern and Cominform, has had 25 meetings held in various Latin American capitals. Bringing together most of the parties and movements of the radical left, not only from the Americas, but also from all over the world, the SPF is much more than a choreographed showcase for a jovial festivity that brings together the ultra-left and is full of anti-capitalist speeches, with its declarations and socialist chanting, and rationalizations. That is what the meetings are for: to project an image loaded with symbolism, to ideologically reinforce communism as a viable and sustainable aspiration, and to provide a fertile recruiting ground for Castro-Communist intelligence. Despite holding meetings in different places, its base is, where it has always been since its foundation, in Havana.

The SPF has its command center in communist Cuba. From there, since the 1990s, Cuban communism reconfigured the methodology to achieve political power. Without the financial support of the USSR, it was necessary to abandon the strategy of rural and urban terrorism, guerrilla warfare, bombs, open kidnappings as methods of struggle so prevalent in the 1960s, 1970s and 1980s. The paradigm of the struggle for political power had to be different. It had to be the Chilean way, the way Salvador Allende used to come to power through the democratic path and once installed, begin the process of communicating the country. As Castro-Communism learned a lot from the Chilean example, to mitigate the potential for failure, the Armed Forces were neutralized by different mechanisms: accusations of "violations" of human rights, corruption, forced retirements, etc. Since the 1990s, we see how the Armed Forces were systematically defenestrated in several countries that defeated subversive attempts to collapse the existing order.

The seeds planted by the Cuban dictatorship saw their fruits in the 2000s with the rise of the dictatorial model that sprouted from the SPF in Venezuela, Nicaragua, Ecuador, Bolivia, Brazil, Argentina, Paraguay, and a good number of governments subordinated to the so-called socialism of the 21st century, a version of the real socialism of the 20th century with cosmetic, logistical, and practical adjustments. When we look at the record of the communist war for power in Latin America between 1959 and 1990, all the conquests of international communism in the American continent were reversed, except for Cuba. However, that has not been the case with the dictatorial model of the SPF and its strategic approach based on the methodological reformulation of communism. The list of captive countries has been much longer since this new mode of usurping and retaining power began to be used. The exceptions to the countries that managed to escape the clutches of this dictatorial pattern were those where the Armed Forces were not defenestrated or co-opted.

What must be done to rescue continental democracy? Elementary. Remember what worked and use it wisely. If the decades of struggle against communism was a success from the 1960s to the 1980s (it was), then we must learn from the past, avoid its excesses, but embrace what worked. The nature of communism has not changed. What has changed is the methodology democracies have employed to confront them, defeat them and preserve republican order and open societies. The response must not only be warlike, but ideological, economic, and cultural as well.

Julio M. Shiling

How the Sao Paulo Forum's Dictatorial Model Became Mainstream

Colombia now has a communist president. Petro was among the first Marxist insurgents to heed Castro's call.

The history of Marxist subversion in the Western Hemisphere began as early as 1919. The Bolshevik coup d'état in Russia signified the beginning of a global communist war for political power. Despite successes of the Communist International (Comintern) and Soviet intelligence in destabilizing democratic regimes across the Americas — including penetrating institutions as important as that of various American presidential administrations — victories in the Western Hemisphere were scarce for the most part. The Castro-Communist revolution bolstered socialist expansionism in an unprecedented way after 1959. Ironically, it wasn't until the fall of Soviet communism — thirty-two years later — that socialist despotism began to really blossom in Latin America.

1959 to 1990: Failed Communist Insurgencies

From 1959 to 1990, despite one of the most comprehensive campaigns of communist insurgencies carried out in any part of the world, both rural and urban, the result of communism's war against the existing order was a blatant failure. No country in Latin America was spared the Marxist onslaught. Yet not a socialist dictatorship was in power (except in Cuba) when Soviet communism fell. The reasons for freedom's success in defeating Marxist attempts at overthrowing governments or in rolling back socialist regimes that reached power (Dominican Republic, Chile, Jamaica, Grenada, Nicaragua) were clear. The public forces, including the military, police, and intelligence (domestic and foreign), did a superb job in preventing the formation of and/or uprooting communist dictatorships. Another important factor was a well-seasoned moral and ideological crusade to thwart socialist propaganda throughout those three decades.

Communism and Its Mutations

The fall of the Berlin Wall caused the mutation of communism. Asian communism, that concoction of a Leninist state with a mixed economy and practiced in China and Vietnam, was solidified in the Tiananmen Square massacre of that same year. The post-Soviet Russian regime resulted in a kleptocracy. It used "privatization" schemes to empower former communist and intelligence officers to establish a dictatorship that many refer to today as Putinism. Cultural Marxism, a modern adaptation of Marxist praxis which removed economics and replaced it with culture as a primary determinant in mass consciousness-building and revolution confection (violent or non-violent), has been the post-1989 path to power in established Western democracies. A fourth model, wholly relevant in Latin America, was established at the Sao Paulo Forum (SPF) in 1990.

Unable to access the bountiful resources of the Soviet Union to finance communist belligerent wars any longer, the Castro regime was determined to rescue socialism in Latin America and continue its promotion. The extinct Cuban tyrant recalibrated strategy and developed a dictatorial prototype that could adapt to the circumstances. This required a methodological makeover. Insurgencies would now be carried out by way of mass protests and riots, labor strikes, transportation, and public services interruptions, and other violent modes of societal discourse, all channeled to produce crises. The Marxist insurgents, following the SPF power model, were to compete in competitive elections as "democrats." If or when they won, a systemic deconstruction process was to begin. This was the 21st-century version of a socialist revolution.

The Sao Paulo Forum in Practice: Chile

Constitutional revisionism, castrating the judicial branch, fusing the legislative with the executive, stifling the media, and converting businessmen into regime courtesans was the general blueprint. The most important tactical element in the SPF autocratic game plan was to, either co-opt or defenestrate, the armed forces. There was a logic to this. The prelude to the SPF mechanism was first experimented with in Chile, in 1973.

Salvador Allende followed the same furtive path to socialism that Castro's 1990 scheme called for. It turned out, however, that the military leader the Chilean Marxist placed as head of the armed forces, General Augusto Pinochet, frustrated the Chilean communization project, instead of upholding it. Cuban communism did not want to repeat this mishap and stressed the prioritization of this strategy with the military (co-opt or defenestrate), in its SPF blueprint.

In sharp contrast to the pre-SPF formula, since 1990, fourteen nations have fallen to socialism in Latin America (Venezuela, Nicaragua, Bolivia, Argentina, Uruguay, Paraguay, Brazil, Ecuador, Honduras, El Salvador, Mexico, Peru, Chile, Colombia). Six reversed course

(Argentina, Uruguay, Paraguay, Brazil, Ecuador, Honduras) and two of these returned to the prior SPF power hold status (Argentina, Honduras). The principal factor that contributed to most of those countries that were able to liberate themselves was the military's ability to maintain its integrity (Brazil, Ecuador, Paraguay, Uruguay). Argentina's case was due to the cannibalistic nature of the Peronist factions that cohabit public institutions and the urban/rural political divide.

The Future of Latin America

Colombia now has a communist president. Petro was among the first Marxist insurgents to heed Castro's call to adopt the post-Soviet methodology. The success of the SPF model lies not in the brilliance of the communists, but in the stupidity of the continental democrats. They continue to believe in these disguised terrorists and have failed to elaborate an effective policy to challenge this new variant of socialist subversion. For now, it will depend on the success of the Colombian military to resist the attempt to neutralize its capacity to defend the country. They are now the praetorian guardians of liberty.

ABOUT THE AUTHOR

Julio M. Shiling is a political scientist, author, lecturer, media commentator, columnist, and director of the political forums and digital publications Patria de Martí and The CubanAmerican Voice. He holds a master's degree in political science from Florida International University (FIU) in Miami, Florida, and is a member of The American Political Science Association and the PEN Club of Cuban Writers in Exile.

He is the author of fourteen books, including the much-acclaimed *Dictatorships and Their Paradigms: Why Do Some Dictatorships Fall While Others Do Not?* (2013, 2022), formerly a two-volume work and now formatted into one book. Being fluent in Spanish has allowed him to publish his works in that language as well. His articles and essays have been reproduced in dozens of print and electronic publications in the United States, Latin America, and Europe. As a political scientist and media commentator, he is a frequent guest on local, national, and international television, radio, podcast, and other media platform programs.

Since 2006, Julio M. Shiling has directed Patria de Martí. In 2020, he launched The CubanAmerican Voice, a digital media platform in English. Patria de Martí was awarded the 2015 Human Rights Freedom Award by the Asociación por la Paz Continental (ASOPAZCO), a Spanish NGO dedicated to the promotion of human rights in the world. Additionally, in 2015, he was conferred the Cuban Flag recognition in Boston, Massachusetts, on the celebration of the Grito de Yara. In 2017, he received the Herencia Award from Cuban Cultural Heritage, for his contribution to Cuban culture. He has also founded and managed insurance and financial services companies.

As a lecturer, he regularly participates in forums, conferences, panel discussions, and other public speaking gatherings. In addition, Patria de Martí sponsors "Symposiums for a Free World," a series of conferences designed to promote greater civic awareness bonded to freedom and democracy.

Born in Havana, Cuba, he went into exile with his family at the age of six. After a brief stay in Madrid, Spain, they relocated to the United States, settling in Union City and West New York, both cities in the state of New Jersey. A few years later, they moved to Miami, Florida, where he currently resides.